Contents

No Mandate for Republicans	2
Voters Want Compromise but Don't Expect It	3
Obama's Relationship with the New Congress	4
Prospects for Obama's Agenda in Divided Government	6
Tax Cuts: Extend or Let Expire?	6
Health Care: Will Republicans "Repeal and Replace" New Law?	7
Federal Budget Deficits: How to Reduce the Debt?	9
National Security and Foreign Policy: START and Afghanistan?	9
Energy: Is Renewable the Way?	10
Trade: An Area of Agreement?	11
Transportation: Action Unlikely?	11
Education: Common Ground on Reauthorization?	12
The 2010 Elections: How Republicans Won	12
U.S. House: Largest Republican Gains in Seventy-Two Years	13
U.S. Senate: Republicans Gain, but Fall Short of Majority	18
Republican Wins of Democratic-Held Seats	18
Republicans Hold All of Their Seats	19
Democrats Win Enough to Fend Off GOP Majority	21
Some Senate Setbacks for Republicans	22
Gubernatorial Elections: Republicans Win a Majority	25
State Legislatures	26
Five Reasons Why Democrats Lost	28
Reason #1: The Economy	28
Reason #2: Voter Skepticism toward Obama's Policies	28
Reason #3: History and the "Enthusiasm Gap"	30
Reason #4: Failure to Communicate	32
Reason #5: Outside Spending	32
Notes	34

Midterm Mayhem

What's Next for Obama and the Republicans

Gregory Giroux

CQ PRESS
A Division of SAGE
Washington, D.C.

CQ Press
2300 N Street, NW, Suite 800
Washington, DC 20037

Phone: 202-729-1900; toll-free, 1-866-4CQ-PRESS (1-866-427-7737)

Web: www.cqpress.com

Copyright © 2011 by CQ Press, a division of SAGE. CQ Press is a registered trademark of Congressional Quarterly Inc.

All rights reserved. No part of this publication may be reproduced or transmitted in any form or by any means, electronic or mechanical, including photocopy, recording, or any information storage and retrieval system, without permission in writing from the publisher.

Cover design: Paula Goldstein, Blue Bungalow Design
Composition: C&M Digitals (P) Ltd.
Image credits:
Corbis: 10, 23
GPO Access/Congressional Pictorial Directory: 14 (three images)
Reuters: 1, 15, 20
YouTube: 33

♾ The paper used in this publication exceeds the requirements of the American National Standard for Information Sciences—Permanence of Paper for Printed Library Materials, ANSI Z39.48–1992.

Printed and bound in the United States of America

14 13 12 11 10   1 2 3 4 5

ISBN: 978-1-60871-810-8

OUTLINE:

No Mandate for Republicans

Voters Want Compromise but Don't Expect It

Obama's Relationship with the New Congress

Prospects for Obama's Agenda in Divided Government

The 2010 Elections: How Republicans Won

Five Reasons Why Democrats Lost

The 2010 midterm elections were a setback for President Barack Obama, shown here at a White House press conference the day after elections he referred to as a "shellacking." He said that too many Americans haven't felt the progress he made in his first two years and that the two parties must work together for the common good. The elections, Obama said, "told us . . . that no one party will be able to dictate where we go from here, that we must find common ground . . . in order to make progress on some uncommonly difficult challenges."

The next two years of Barack Obama's term in the White House will be much different than the first two years. Where Obama enjoyed phenomenal legislative successes early in his presidency, the serious setbacks he and the Democratic Party received at the hands of the Republicans in the November 2010 midterm elections will require him to adjust to a political environment of power-sharing.

A "shellacking" is how a chastened Obama, in a press conference November 3—one day after the balloting, described his party's loss of the U.S. House of Representatives and its setbacks in races for the U.S. Senate and for governor. The president accepted some responsibility for his party's defeat.

Voters "understand that I'm the President of the United States, and that my core responsibility is making sure that we've got an economy that's growing, a middle class that feels secure, that jobs are being created," Obama said. "And so I think I've got to take direct responsibility for the fact that we have not made as much progress as we need to make."[1]

But he also maintained that the balloting was not a repudiation of the direction his administration had laid out for the nation in the first two years. Obama said the lesson of the election results was that the public was frustrated with the slow rate of economic recovery and wants the two political parties to work together to solve the country's problems.

"The American people were not issuing a mandate for gridlock," Obama said November 14. "They want to see us make progress because they understand instinctually how competitive things are and how we have to step up our game."[2]

The coming two years will be a major test of President Obama's leadership skills and his ability to "make some mid-course corrections and adjustments," as he said during a trip to Asia after the election. After a two-year period during which a compliant Democratic Congress propelled most of his legislative priorities to passage, Obama must now work with a Republican-controlled House of Representatives—a chamber dominated by conservatives with whom the president does not see eye to eye ideologically.

While the November elections kept the Senate in Democratic hands, the party only controls 53 of the 100 seats—a nominal majority in a slow-moving chamber that effectively requires 60 votes to advance major legislation because of filibuster protections afforded to the minority party. Even when Democrats held 59 or 60 seats in the Senate in 2009 and 2010, it wasn't always easy for Obama to get his agenda through the chamber. It will be much harder now.

Overall, it will be an atypical power structure in Washington for the next two years. Not since the Civil War has there been a combination of a Democratic president, a Republican-controlled House, and a Democratic-run Senate.

No Mandate for Republicans

While ecstatic over their big wins in the House and Senate, Republicans said after the election that they didn't interpret the results as a mandate for their party. It is clear from polling data that the Republican Party prevailed in the 2010 election despite its public image, not because of it.

According to an exit poll of tens of thousands of voters, 42 percent of respondents said they had a favorable view of the Republican Party, and 52 percent said they had an unfavorable view. For the Democrats, the figures were nearly the same—43 percent favorable and 53 percent unfavorable.[3]

Republicans noted that they held congressional majorities in the House and Senate as recently as 2006, and they had learned from their failures to make Congress responsive to the public and honor promises to streamline government. "Tea Party" activists who propelled Republicans to a House majority will be disappointed and may sit out the 2012 election if Republicans don't deliver in the next two years.

Marco Rubio, a Florida Republican who was elected to the Senate, said in the Republicans' national radio address four days after the election that "we Republicans would be mistaken if we misread these results as simply an embrace of the Republican Party."

"This election is a second chance—a second chance for Republicans to be what we said we were going to be," Rubio stated.[4]

"I think the Republican Party needs to understand that if we don't keep the promises that we made to the American people that they will fire us again," said Raul Labrador, an Idaho Republican, after he defeated one-term Democratic representative Walt Minnick.[5]

Republican gains owed less to what the candidates proposed to do and more to historical trends and what voters disliked about what the Democratic-run government was doing. At the time of the election, most Americans didn't have a clear idea of what the Republicans stood for, other than they were not incumbent-party Democrats.

In late September, Republicans introduced their "Pledge to America," a campaign manifesto that included promises to end federal "bailouts," repeal the Democratic-written health care law, and cut taxes. The document didn't get much attention (in part because Obama was addressing the United Nations in New York City at exactly the same time Republicans were rolling out their plan at a hardware store in northern Virginia), and there is no evidence it influenced public opinion. As one Republican campaign consultant told *Washington Post* political journalist Chris Cillizza after the election: "[I]f we didn't have the Pledge to America, we would have picked up the exact same number of seats . . . it didn't get or lose us a vote."[6]

Voters Want Compromise but Don't Expect It

Most Americans want the two parties to work together but are not confident they will. According to an Associated Press survey taken right after the election, 41 percent of respondents said they were confident that President Obama and congressional Republicans "can work together to solve the country's problems." Fifty-eight percent said they were not confident the two parties can work together.[7]

In an era of divided government, compromise will be necessary to implement major changes in policy. The results of the 2010 election will require a mid-course pivot from Obama, who cannot pass any bills in the House or Senate without Republican support. Governing with a Republican House will test the leadership style of Obama, a former state legislator and U.S. senator who never served in an executive capacity prior to his election as president.

"I think several things can get done, but he has to demonstrate that he really understands the art of governing and reaching out, rather than the art of campaigning, which is just demolishing and demonizing people," Kenneth Duberstein, a former chief of staff to President Ronald Reagan who supported Obama in the 2008 presidential election, said in mid-October on Bloomberg Television.[8]

Most Americans think that Obama is more compromise-minded than the Republicans. According to a *USA Today*/Gallup poll taken immediately after the election, 64 percent of respondents said that Obama would "make a sincere effort to work with the Republicans in Congress to find solutions that are acceptable to both parties." Just 43 percent said that congressional Republicans would make a sincere effort to work with Obama.[9]

Many political analysts and Congress-watchers are predicting more gridlock than cooperation. Obama and the Republicans generally do not see eye to eye on major issues such as how to boost the economy and expand health care coverage. Obama has indicated that he will resist Republican efforts to rescind unspent money in the 2009 federal stimulus law and repeal the 2010 health care law.

In addition, there are fewer Obama allies in Congress and few compromise-minded moderates. Nearly half of the Blue Dog Coalition, a group of about fifty centrist Democrats who promote fiscal restraint, lost in the elections. This effectively made the Democratic House caucus more liberal. Dozens of Tea Party–affiliated conservative Republicans first elected to Congress in 2010 ran as opponents of the Obama administration and are more likely to confront the president on policy than to compromise with him.

"I've been willing to compromise in the past, and I am willing to compromise going forward on a whole range of issues," Obama said November 3, the day after the election, at the same White House press conference mentioned earlier. "There are some areas where it's going to be very difficult for us to agree."

Obama's Relationship with the New Congress

In 2009 and 2010, Obama had the advantage of governing with a friendly Democratic Congress that used its huge seat advantage over Republicans to pass bills the administration wanted. The new Republican-run House will be a major roadblock to the administration and will scrutinize the administration's policies and writing of federal regulations more closely than the Democrats have done recently.

Obama could have a confrontational relationship with House Republicans, who have made clear they will use the congressional oversight process to grill administration officials and point out what Republicans see as excesses in administration policy.

Representative Darrell Issa, a California Republican, will become chair of the House Oversight and Government Reform Committee, the principal investigative committee in the House and an influential panel that has the power to call hearings and issue subpoenas. He could be a constant thorn in Obama's side.

"I'm going to go after a lot of things, and I'm going to do a lot of investigating," Issa said a few days after the election.[10]

Former New York Republican representative James Walsh said that he expected Issa to be an aggressive chair in the mold of Henry Waxman, the California Democrat

U.S. House Republicans to Watch in the 112th Congress

JOHN BOEHNER, *Ohio*—Boehner's elevation to House Speaker, second in the presidential line of succession, marks a remarkable comeback for the ten-term Republican. Boehner lost a party leadership position after the 1998 elections in which Republicans lost seats. He concentrated on his work on the Education and Labor Committee and then returned to the leadership in 2006, when he became majority leader after Tom DeLay of Texas stepped down from the post. After Democrats won the majority in the 2006 election, Boehner served as minority leader for four years.

DARRELL ISSA, *California*—Issa, who won a sixth term in November to a Republican-leaning district in southern California, will become chair of the House Government Reform and Oversight Committee. Look for a parade of Obama administration officials to appear before his investigative committee.

PAUL RYAN, *Wisconsin*—Just forty when he won a seventh term in November, Ryan is now a veteran of Congress who racked up enough seniority to become chair of the Budget Committee, a natural fit for this number-crunching former congressional aide. He will continue to be a leading voice in debates over how to bring federal revenues in line with expenditures. Democrats and liberals oppose his budget policies but credit him with putting forward serious proposals.

DAVE CAMP, *Michigan*—Camp will head the Ways and Means Committee, an influential panel that has jurisdiction over tax and trade policy, Social Security, and Medicare. The major changes Republicans want to make to the health care overhaul must be vetted by Ways and Means. Camp has rejected any deficit reduction plan that includes tax increases and wants to extend tax reductions to all Americans regardless of income level.

---

who headed the oversight committee from 2007 to 2009 and used his powers to probe George W. Bush's administration on climate change, the subprime mortgage crisis, and other issues.[11]

Fred Upton, a Michigan Republican who sought the chairmanship of the Energy and Commerce Committee, said that the Democratic-controlled Congress did not vet the Obama administration's proposals as rigorously as it did Bush administration's proposals. Upton would keep a watchful eye on Environmental Protection Agency regulations he says are too costly for business.

Issa, Upton, and other Republicans have also made clear they want to examine the many "czars" that Obama appointed to oversee administration policy on specific issues and who are not subject to Senate confirmation.

"It is time to hold them accountable for what they are trying to promulgate with rules and regulations," Upton said just before the election.[12]

The 2010 election results should compel Obama to take a compromise-minded approach in the Senate, where the Republicans' 6-seat gain strengthened the hand of minority leader Mitch McConnell. He will lead forty-seven Republicans in a chamber that essentially requires just 40 votes to block action. So Obama will not be able to enact major legislation without some Republican support in the Senate.

Throughout 2009 and 2010, Republicans used the threat of a filibuster to effectively force the Democrats to schedule cloture votes and achieve 60-vote supermajorities to enact legislation. For example, on Christmas Eve 2009 the Senate passed the health care overhaul, 60–39, only after it voted to invoke cloture, or cut off debate, on the bill.[13]

In the new Congress, the Democrats won't have the luxury of advancing legislation even if they all vote together against united Republican opposition.

The new Senate could see an increase in clout and visibility for the most politically centrist conservative Republican senators, namely Olympia J. Snowe and Susan Collins of Maine, who sometimes vote with the Democrats.

Compromise-minded Republican senators up for re-election in 2012 may come under pressure to vote more in line with conservative positions so as to avoid reprisals in primary elections from challengers affiliated with the Tea Party. Snowe and Texas senator Kay Bailey Hutchison are just two Republicans who could face serious primary challenges in the 2012 election if they seek re-election.

And Democrats can't expect a united caucus on all major votes. Some moderate and conservative Democrats may be hesitant to side too frequently with Obama, especially if his approval rating does not improve. For example, Ben Nelson of Nebraska, who is probably the least liberal Democratic senator, is up for re-election in 2012 in a Republican-leaning state that gave Obama just 42 percent of the vote in 2008.

Prospects for Obama's Agenda in Divided Government

So will a Democratic president up for re-election in 2012, a Senate narrowly controlled by Democrats, and a House strongly controlled by Republicans be able to agree on anything?

After the election, Obama and Republicans began sketching out some of their policy priorities for the next two years. They could find some common ground on energy, trade, and education policy, but they remain far apart on tax and health care policy and more generally separated on the proper role of the federal government in promoting economic growth.

Here's a look at the prospects for bipartisanship on some major issues Obama and the new Congress will tackle:

Tax Cuts: Extend or Let Expire?

Both President Obama and congressional Republicans want to extend soon-to-expire tax cuts to boost a fragile economy that continues to be hampered by an unemployment rate near 10 percent.

But Obama and Republicans disagree on which of the tax cuts should be extended. Obama and most Democrats call for extending lower tax rates for individuals making less than $200,000 per year and families making less than $250,000 per year. They don't want to extend the cuts for the wealthy because it would exacerbate budget deficits.

Obama said November 6 that he recognized that "both parties are going to have to work together and compromise to get something done here. But I want to make my priorities clear from the start. One: middle-class families need permanent tax relief. And two: I believe we can't afford to borrow and spend another $700 billion on permanent tax cuts for millionaires and billionaires."[14]

Republicans want all of the tax cuts extended before they expire December 31, 2010, regardless of income threshold. They say that upper-income earners include entrepreneurs and businesses that create jobs.

Obama administration officials said that they are willing to compromise with Republicans. One potential area of agreement: extending the cuts indefinitely for most taxpayers and keeping lower rates for wealthy taxpayers for a set period of time, perhaps one to three years.

According to a national poll taken October 7–10, 2010, 43 percent of respondents agreed with Obama's position and 34 percent sided with the Republican position. Twenty percent said that the tax cuts should expire as scheduled and the added revenue used to reduce the deficit.[15] According to another national poll, this one taken just after the November elections, 53 percent of respondents said that the tax cuts should continue for everyone and 32 percent said that the tax cuts should expire for persons making more than $250,000 but should continue for everyone else.[16]

Health Care: Will Republicans "Repeal and Replace" New Law?

Obama will confront a Republican-run House intent on repealing and replacing the health care overhaul. He may need to ready his veto pen.

Obama has defended the law, which will set up a system of health insurance "exchanges" in which uninsured Americans can compare and purchase health plans. The law bars insurance companies from denying coverage based on pre-existing conditions and also prevents insurers from implementing lifetime caps on coverage.

Most Democrats voted for the bill as an improvement over the status quo. No Republican voted for the measure, which party members said was too bureaucratic and would not contain rising health care costs.

The American people are divided on the question of repeal: according to a national poll in early October, 47 percent said that the bill should be repealed and 42 percent said it should not be repealed.

Yet when respondents were told of eight major provisions in the law, majorities said that six of the provisions should be kept. By a 75 percent to 24 percent margin, respondents supported a provision that prohibits insurance companies from denying coverage based on pre-existing conditions. Those surveyed also backed, by a

67 percent to 32 percent margin, a provision that allows children to remain on their parents' policies up to age 26.

A poll conducted October 5–10 for the Kaiser Family Foundation said that Americans were "chronically divided" over the health care law, though their feelings about it "are not a dominant factor in how they will vote for Congress or whether they will go to the polls." The survey showed that just 10 percent of respondents identified health care as the most important issue in their vote for Congress, well behind the 35 percent who said the economy and jobs. Additionally, 63 percent said the passage of the new law would not affect their vote.[17]

Repeal may be a moot point because Republicans and some conservative Democrats who opposed the bill don't have the votes to fully repeal the legislation. President Obama, by the power of the presidential veto, will be able to block anything that doesn't receive a two-thirds vote in Congress. The president made clear just before and after the election that he would vigorously defend the new law.

"What's going to be tested after the election is these specific provisions and how do they feel about them?" Obama said in an interview with *National Journal*, a Washington-based publication, about two weeks before the election. "Because it turns out that those provisions are hugely popular and they're the right thing to do."

The president also said that Republicans are "going to have to answer the fact" that, according to the Congressional Budget Office, "implementing health care will save us a trillion dollars over the course of two decades."

"They will have to answer where we're going to make up that trillion dollars, and how do they square that with their claim that they want to balance the budget," he said.[18]

Senate majority leader Harry Reid, D-NV, said the day after the election that "if there's some tweaking to do with the health care bill, I'm ready for some tweaking." But he said Congress should not substantially rework a bill he said did "great things."[19]

Senate minority leader Mitch McConnell, a Kentucky Republican, said two days after the election that "we can and should propose and vote on straight repeal repeatedly," even though Republicans don't have the votes to override a presidential veto. Still, Republicans want to test Democrats' commitment to the legislation and force Democrats seeking re-election in 2012 to defend the new law.

Short of repealing the health care law, Republicans will use the appropriations process to try to stall its implementation or withhold federal funds to carry out the law. Just before the election, Republicans suggested that they might try to defund key parts of the measure.

"If all of Obamacare cannot be immediately repealed, then it is my intention to begin repealing it piece by piece, blocking funding for its implementation and blocking the issuance of the regulations necessary to implement it," Virginia representative Eric Cantor, the incoming House majority leader, said after the election.[20]

Federal Budget Deficits: How to Reduce the Debt?

Obama and congressional Democrats and Republicans all have expressed concern about huge federal budget deficits and the national debt, which was more than $13.7 trillion in November 2010. Both parties want to reduce the debt but have different philosophies regarding how to do it.

There was an increased focus in the 2010 election on the federal debt and the deficit in part because of the influence of Tea Party activists who advocate restraint in federal spending.

In February 2010, Obama signed an executive order establishing the National Commission on Fiscal Responsibility and Reform, a bipartisan panel that was tasked with "identifying policies to improve the fiscal situation in the medium term and to achieve fiscal responsibility over the long run." Of its eighteen members, six were appointed by Obama and three apiece by House Speaker Nancy Pelosi, House minority leader John Boehner, Senate majority leader Harry Reid and Senate minority leader Mitch McConnell.[21]

The panel planned to vote on a final report by December 1, 2010. Less than three weeks prior to that, commission cochairs Erskine Bowles, a former chief of staff to President Bill Clinton, and Alan Simpson, a former Republican senator from Wyoming, introduced a proposal that called for a mix of tax increases and spending reductions to close the budget gap as well as a gradual increase in the eligibility age to receive Social Security benefits.

Republicans are likely to resist tax increases in a debt reduction plan, and many Democrats and liberal groups said an increase in the retirement age is a nonstarter. Pelosi said the Bowles-Simpson plan was "simply unacceptable." Obama hasn't endorsed any particular approach.

"Before anybody starts shooting down proposals, I think we need to listen. We need to gather up all the facts," Obama said after the Bowles-Simpson plan was released. He also said, "[I]f we are concerned about debt and deficits we're going to have to take actions that are difficult and we're going to have to tell the truth to the American people."[22]

National Security and Foreign Policy: START and Afghanistan?

One of Obama's top foreign policy goals was to enact a new nuclear arms treaty with Russia before the end of 2010. Obama said in mid-November 2010 that the Senate's ratification of the new Strategic Arms Reduction Treaty (START) "is a national security imperative."[23]

Republicans pushed back against Obama, saying that the issues were too complex to resolve before year's end. Arizona senator Jon Kyl, the number two Republican in the chamber, wants the Obama administration to commit more money to modernizing the U.S. nuclear arsenal before Kyl endorses the treaty.

The *New York Times* said the "make or break battle" over the treaty "could be an early test of [Obama's] mettle heading into the final two years of his term."[24]

One issue that will command the attention of Democrats and Republicans is reducing the national debt, which was more than $13.7 trillion in November 2010. In February 2010 President Obama signed an executive order creating the National Commission on Fiscal Responsibility and Reform; he is pictured here with Vice President Joe Biden and panel cochairs Erskine Bowles, a former chief of staff to President Bill Clinton, and Alan Simpson (far right), a former Republican senator from Wyoming. The commission was expected to produce recommendations in December that included a mixture of spending reductions and tax hikes that will be difficult to pass in Congress.

It may be more difficult to enact the treaty in 2011, when the Democratic majority will shrink by six, to fifty-three (the total includes two independents who caucus with the party). A two-thirds vote is required to ratify the treaty.

The U.S. war in Afghanistan entered its tenth year in late 2010, and Obama and Republicans generally see eye to eye on a military strategy to rid the country of al-Qaeda terrorists. Republicans do oppose tentative deadlines to begin withdrawing troops, even as some antiwar Democratic liberals are uneasy with the large U.S. military presence in Afghanistan.

Energy: Is Renewable the Way?

Republican gains in the election will require Obama to take a different tack on energy and climate change policy.

There is no chance of reviving a "cap and trade" energy bill to reduce greenhouse gases that the Democratic-run House narrowly passed in 2009 but which stalled in the Senate. "Cap and trade is gone" and is "finished for now," Sen. John Kerry, a Massachusetts Democrat, said after the election.

Obama and Republicans could find common ground on a revised energy bill that would boost renewable-energy production and efficiency. Republicans will push for increased offshore drilling in any energy proposal. Like many Republicans, Obama supports increased use of nuclear power.

Trade: An Area of Agreement?

Trade might be an area of agreement between Obama and the Republicans. A Republican-controlled House could breathe new life into free trade agreements with Colombia, Panama, and South Korea that President George W. Bush completed but which were never ratified in a Democratic-run Congress.

In his 2010 State of the Union address, Obama said that "we will strengthen our trade relations in Asia and with key partners like South Korea and Panama and Colombia," though the agreements languished in a Congress controlled by Democrats, many of whom are close to labor unions that feel free trade agreements abrogate environmental and labor standards.[25]

"I think the president has to take a lead on trade and the free trade agreements," Kenneth Duberstein said on Bloomberg Television in mid-October.[26]

Doug Pinkham, president of the Public Affairs Council, said after the election that he hoped "we can have a more adult conversation" about trade, which "is very important to economic growth in this country."

"And if we can have some more adult conversations about trade agreements and about the ability of our very capable manufacturing sector to supply products and get them in markets around the world, that would certainly be a good thing," Pinkham continued.[27]

The public has a mixed view on trade pacts. According to a national survey conducted November 4–7 by the Pew Research Center for the People and the Press, 35 percent said that free trade agreements have been good for the United States, while 44 percent of respondents said that they have been bad for the country. Just 28 percent of Republicans said that trade pacts were good for the country, down from 43 percent in November 2009. Most respondents said that increased trade with Canada, Japan, India, and European Union countries would be good for the United States, though they have mixed views about increased trade with South Korea and China.[28]

Transportation: Action Unlikely?

There is no disagreement among Democrats and Republicans that the nation's transportation infrastructure is in need of improvement—or that such investments would help create jobs at a time when so many individuals are looking for work. But huge budget deficits and a bipartisan aversion to tax hikes will make it unlikely that Congress will significantly boost transportation spending in 2011 or 2012.

The new House Republican majority could make it difficult for Obama to enact a $50 billion transportation spending program he introduced in October 2010. John Mica, the incoming chair of the House Transportation and Infrastructure Committee, described the proposal as "a pitiful and tardy political excuse" and said it was "astounding" that the administration would call for spending $50 billion when so much of the infrastructure dollars in the economic stimulus plan remain unspent.[29]

Senators Tom Carper, a Delaware Democrat, and George Voinovich, an Ohio Republican who did not seek re-election in 2010, proposed in November 2010 that the national gas tax be increased by 25 cents over a three-year period to replenish the federal Highway Trust Fund that funds transportation improvements. The tax rate has been unchanged since 1993, when it was raised by 4.3 cents.

The senators said that their proposal would raise $200 billion over five years. They would devote $117 billion to transportation improvements and $83 billion for deficit reduction.

But neither Republicans nor the Obama administration want to raise fuel taxes.

"In an environment where you are trying to control spending, where Republicans are viscerally opposed to raising taxes of any kind and where the incumbent Democratic president continues to signal his opposition to fuel taxes, I don't know of any scenario that would lead me to believe that there's a snowball's chance in hell that you're going to pass a multiyear surface transportation bill," said Jim Burney, a former U.S. transportation secretary. "I don't see that happening until at least 2013."[30]

Education: Common Ground on Reauthorization?

Obama could find some common ground with Republicans on a reauthorization of the 2002 No Child Left Behind education law. Education secretary Arne Duncan said in November 2010 that he was working with incoming Republican House Speaker John Boehner on revisions to the law, which provides federal aid to public schools and requires states to assess students' skills through standardized tests.[31]

Obama has also called for more federal funding for U.S. community colleges, which he described in an October 2010 speech as the "unsung heroes" of the U.S. educational system. The Obama administration has a goal of making the United States the top-ranking country in the world in percentage of college graduates by 2020.[32]

"If we are not able to produce more scientists and more engineers, and more highly skilled technical workers, then other countries are going to clean our clock," the president told *National Journal* two weeks before the election.[33]

The 2010 Elections: How Republicans Won

It was not a great time to be a Democratic incumbent in 2010. Voters were angry about the poor economy and took out their frustration on Democrats.

Many Americans, including political independents, soured on the ability of the Democratic Party to produce change as promised in the 2006 and 2008 elections. In October 2010, Gallup found that 40 percent of respondents agreed with the statement that Democrats "can bring about the changes this country needs." That was down from 59 percent in October 2006, just before the Democrats won control of Congress.

This is not to say that the voting public has great affection for the Republicans. On the question of whether the Republican Party "can bring about the changes this country needs," 43 percent of respondents said that applied to the party, barely higher than the 40 percent 2010 Democratic score and the identical 2006 Republican score.[34]

By the time the November 2 elections approached, there was a clear consensus that Republicans would win control of the House and make gains in the Senate. Larry J. Sabato, the director of the University of Virginia's Center for Politics, wrote on September 2 that "Republicans have a good chance to win the House by picking up as many as 47 seats, net."[35] In an updated prediction just before the election, Sabato upped that number to 55 seats.

Charlie Cook, founder of *The Cook Political Report* newsletter and a prominent election forecaster, wrote on September 28 that "it seems extremely likely that the GOP will regain control of the House, but it is less clear whether this election is headed for net seat gains in the 40s or 50s or if the number will be even higher." In the Senate, Cook wrote that "we could see Republican gains of seven or eight seats, but they could be as high as nine or 10."[36]

U.S. House: Largest Republican Gains in Seventy-Two Years

The Republicans made a net gain of at least 63 seats in the U.S. House elections, far more than the 39 they needed to overcome the Democrats' 255–178 advantage on election day. (There were two vacancies on election day, one in a Democratic-held district and one in a Republican-held district.)

Republicans unseated at least fifty-two Democratic incumbents and were set to begin the new Congress with as many as 243 seats, the most since they had 246 seats at the beginning of the 80th Congress in 1947. The Republican gains in the House were the party's largest since the 1938 election, when they gained more than 80 seats at the midpoint of Democratic president Franklin D. Roosevelt's second term.

A Democratic incumbent trailed in one other contest that was still too close to call in late November, so overall Republican gains could reach 64 seats.

Republicans made gains all over the nation and particularly in the Midwest and South. The Republican defeated five Democratic incumbents in Ohio and four apiece in Florida, Illinois, and Pennsylvania. They won 2 seats in Arkansas, long a bastion of conservative Democratic politics, and 3 in Tennessee.

About two-thirds of the House Democrats who lost were first elected in either 2006, when Democrats won control of Congress, or in 2008, when Obama's election helped Democrats solidify their majorities. This group included Alan Grayson, a Florida Democrat first elected in 2008 who drew national attention for his aggressive rhetoric against Republican policies. Seeking re-election in anti-Democrat 2010, Grayson was defeated by eighteen percentage points.

Yet even some veteran Democrats were swept away in the Republican wave of 2010. The victims included three committee chairs with nearly a century of combined congressional service: Jim Oberstar of Minnesota, John Spratt of South Carolina, and Ike Skelton of Missouri. In southwestern Virginia, fourteen-term incumbent Rick Boucher had such a seeming lock on his district that the Republicans didn't field a candidate against him in 2008. But he too was defeated for re-election in 2010 by a serious Republican candidate.

The 2010 elections saw the defeat of some long-serving Democratic members of the House of Representatives, including chairs of influential committees. Jim Oberstar of Minnesota, chair of the Transportation and Infrastructure Committee (left); Ike Skelton of Missouri, chair of the Armed Services Committee (center); and John Spratt of South Carolina, head of the Budget Committee (right), were all defeated. Together, they had served 98 years in Congress.

As bad as the House elections were for Democrats, there's evidence to suggest it could have been a lot worse. In the waning weeks of the campaign, officials at the Democratic Congressional Campaign Committee (DCCC), the campaign arm of House Democrats, focused their advertising dollars on races in which Republican challengers were making late surges. The DCCC didn't spend money on races in which their candidates were likely to lose decisively, even if they were incumbent officeholders.

For example, the DCCC didn't spend any money to help re-elect Illinois Democratic representative Debbie Halvorson, a first-term member who lost by fifteen percentage points to Republican challenger Adam Kinzinger. The DCCC felt that its resources were better spent in winnable contests, such as in the race for the northern Virginia district of Democratic representative Gerry Connolly. He won a very close race in part because the DCCC spent $1.6 million attacking his Republican opponent.

Had the DCCC spent less money on Connolly's race and used those funds to help Halvorson, both Democrats may have lost.

Maryland representative Chris Van Hollen, who oversaw party strategy and spending in the 2010 elections as DCCC chair, said in a post-election memorandum that his operation "recognized that it would have to manage its resources to respond to late-breaking races in an expanding playing field."

"To provide flexibility, the DCCC made some very wrenching and tough decisions regarding resource allocation," Van Hollen wrote. "While painful, these decisions ensured we had finances available to defend many members from the onslaught of outside spending in the final weeks of the election."[37]

Some Republican strategists said after the election that the party might have won more seats if the Republican National Committee (RNC), which underperformed in fund-raising under the rocky leadership of Michael Steele, had been able to fully fund its voter turnout programs. Two weeks after the election, RNC political director

Ohio Republican representative John A. Boehner speaks to reporters at a news conference November 3, 2010, one day after sweeping Republican gains in U.S. House elections positioned him to become the next Speaker of the House. Boehner is flanked by Sen. Mitch McConnell, a Kentucky Republican who will lead a larger Senate minority of forty-seven Republicans (left), and Mississippi governor Haley Barbour, chair of the Republican Governors Association and a key player in his party's efforts to secure more governorships ahead of congressional redistricting in 2011 and 2012.

Gentry Collins, in a detailed memorandum announcing his resignation, said 21 more Democratic House seats "could have been competitive if not for lack of funds."[38]

Still, the Republican gains were more than sufficient to make John Boehner the next Speaker of the House. A twenty-year House member from southwestern Ohio, Boehner served as chair of the House Republican Conference in the 1990s and headed the Education and the Workforce Committee (now Education and Labor) from 2001 to 2006. He served briefly as majority leader in 2006 and as minority leader from 2007 through 2010.

Rep. Eric Cantor of Virginia will become majority leader, the number two spot, and will assist Boehner in setting the Republican Party's agenda and strategy. Rep. Kevin McCarthy of California, who headed candidate recruitment efforts for Republicans in the 2010 election, will become majority whip, the number three position.

Boehner will replace California Democratic representative Nancy Pelosi, who became the first woman Speaker just four years ago. Pelosi chose to run for minority leader, the top Democratic slot in the opposition—and this move was a surprise to some political analysts, who expected that she would step down from her post after her party's losses.

J. Dennis Hastert, her predecessor as Speaker, did not run for minority leader after the Republicans lost their majority in the 2006 election. Hastert resigned from

TABLE 1
Congressional Incumbents Defeated in 2010 General Election

Senate (2 Democrats)

Name	Party	State	Terms Served	Challenger
Blanche Lincoln	Democrat	Arkansas	2	John Boozman
Russ Feingold	Democrat	Wisconsin	3	Ron Johnson

House (52 Democrats, 2 Republicans)

Name	Party	State and District	Terms Served	Challenger
Bobby Bright	Democrat	Alabama's 2nd	1	Martha Roby
Ann Kirkpatrick	Democrat	Arizona's 1st	1	Paul Gosar
Harry Mitchell	Democrat	Arizona's 5th	2	David Schweikert
John Salazar	Democrat	Colorado's 3rd	3	Scott Tipton
Betsy Markey	Democrat	Colorado's 4th	1	Cory Gardner
Allen Boyd	Democrat	Florida's 2nd	7	Steve Southerland
Alan Grayson	Democrat	Florida's 8th	1	Dan Webster
Ron Klein	Democrat	Florida's 22nd	2	Allen West
Suzanne Kosmas	Democrat	Florida's 24th	1	Sandy Adams
Jim Marshall	Democrat	Georgia's 8th	4	Austin Scott
Charles Djou	Republican	Hawaii's 1st	1*	Colleen Hanabusa
Walt Minnick	Democrat	Idaho's 1st	1	Raul Labrador
Melissa Bean	Democrat	Illinois's 8th	3	Joe Walsh
Debbie Halvorson	Democrat	Illinois's 11th	1	Adam Kinzinger
Bill Foster	Democrat	Illinois's 14th	1	Randy Hultgren
Phil Hare	Democrat	Illinois's 17th	2	Bobby Schilling
Baron Hill	Democrat	Indiana's 9th	5**	Todd Young
Anh "Joseph" Cao	Republican	Louisiana's 2nd	1	Cedric Richmond
Frank Kratovil	Democrat	Maryland's 1st	1	Andy Harris
Mark Schauer	Democrat	Michigan's 7th	1	Tim Walberg
Jim Oberstar	Democrat	Minnesota's 8th	18	Chip Cravaack
Travis Childers	Democrat	Mississippi's 1st	1	Alan Nunnelee
Gene Taylor	Democrat	Mississippi's 4th	10	Steven Palazzo
Ike Skelton	Democrat	Missouri's 4th	17	Vicky Hartzler
Dina Titus	Democrat	Nevada's 3rd	1	Joe Heck
Carol Shea-Porter	Democrat	New Hampshire's 1st	2	Frank Guinta
John Adler	Democrat	New Jersey's 3rd	1	Jon Runyan
Harry Teague	Democrat	New Mexico's 2nd	1	Steve Pearce
Michael McMahon	Democrat	New York's 13th	1	Michael Grimm
John Hall	Democrat	New York's 19th	2	Nan Hayworth
Scott Murphy	Democrat	New York's 20th	1*	Chris Gibson
Michael Arcuri	Democrat	New York's 24th	2	Richard Hanna
Dan Maffei	Democrat	New York's 25th	1	Ann Marie Buerkle
Bob Etheridge	Democrat	North Carolina's 2nd	7	Renee Ellmers
Earl Pomeroy	Democrat	North Dakota's At-Large	9	Rick Berg

Midterm Mayhem

House (52 Democrats, 2 Republicans)

Name	Party	State and District	Terms Served	Challenger
Steve Driehaus	Democrat	Ohio's 1st	1	Steve Chabot
Charlie Wilson	Democrat	Ohio's 6th	2	Bill Johnson
Mary Jo Kilroy	Democrat	Ohio's 15th	1	Steve Stivers
John Boccieri	Democrat	Ohio's 16th	1	Jim Renacci
Zack Space	Democrat	Ohio's 18th	2	Bob Gibbs
Kathy Dahlkemper	Democrat	Pennsylvania's 3rd	1	Mike Kelly
Patrick Murphy	Democrat	Pennsylvania's 8th	2	Mike Fitzpatrick
Chris Carney	Democrat	Pennsylvania's 10th	2	Tom Marino
Paul Kanjorski	Democrat	Pennsylvania's 11th	13	Lou Barletta
John Spratt	Democrat	South Carolina's 5th	14	Mick Mulvaney
Stephanie Herseth Sandlin	Democrat	South Dakota's At-Large	3	Kristi Noem
Lincoln Davis	Democrat	Tennessee's 4th	4	Scott DesJarlais
Chet Edwards	Democrat	Texas's 17th	10	Bill Flores
Ciro Rodriguez	Democrat	Texas's 23rd	5**	Quico Canseco
Solomon Ortiz	Democrat	Texas's 27th	14	Blake Farenthold
Glenn Nye	Democrat	Virginia's 2nd	1	Scott Rigell
Tom Perriello	Democrat	Virginia's 5th	1	Robert Hurt
Rick Boucher	Democrat	Virginia's 9th	14	Morgan Griffith
Steve Kagen	Democrat	Wisconsin's 8th	2	Reid Ribble

Source: Compiled by the author.
Note: Democratic representative Tim Bishop (New York's 1st district) was in a contest still too close to call as of November 24, 2010.
*Murphy won a special election in March 2009, and Djou won a special election in May 2010. **Hill and Rodriguez served two non-consecutive tenures.

Congress in late 2007, and some speculated that Pelosi might even resign her seat to avoid being a distraction for dispirited Democrats.

Tim Holden, a moderate Democrat from Pennsylvania, said after the election that Pelosi "drove the bus . . . off the Grand Canyon" and that "I don't think she should be the leader of the Democratic Party."[39]

Yet when Democrats held leadership elections two weeks after the midterms, Pelosi easily won the minority leader's race by a vote of 150–43 over Heath Shuler of North Carolina, a member of the Blue Dog Coalition of Democrats who support fiscal restraint and are less liberal than Pelosi. Shuler argued that Democrats needed to take a different tack after their losses and elect a leader who is more popular with independent voters. He said that he ran to "ensure that the moderates are heard."[40]

Though the Democrats lost control of the House on Pelosi's watch, the defeat of so many moderate and conservative Democrats actually made it easier for her to stay on as the leader of a Democratic caucus that is mostly liberal and loyal to her. About one in six House Democrats in the new Congress is from California alone.

U.S. Senate: Republicans Gain, but Fall Short of Majority

In the Senate, the Republicans made a net gain of 6 seats to narrow the Democrats' advantage to 53–47. The Republicans defeated two Democratic incumbents, Russ Feingold of Wisconsin and Blanche Lincoln of Arkansas, and also won seats in Illinois, Indiana, North Dakota, and Pennsylvania that Democratic incumbents were not defending. No Republican-held seat went Democratic.

The Republican gains will give the party a bigger say over the legislative agenda in 2011 and 2012 and position members for a potential takeover of the Senate in 2012, when twenty-three Democratic senators (including two independents) and just ten Republican senators are up for re-election. The reason for that partisan disparity is that Democrats won a disproportionate number of the Senate races in 2006 and therefore have so many seats to defend. Not since the 1980 election has the partisan distribution of Senate seats on the ballot been as lopsided.

Here's a closer look at some of the key races:

> **FUN FACT**
>
> The 2010 election was the third consecutive balloting in which all of the Senate seats that saw a change in party control were in the same partisan direction. Six Senate seats flipped from Democratic to Republican control in 2010 (and none from Republican to Democratic); 8 seats flipped from Republican to Democratic in 2008; and 6 seats went from Democratic to Republican.

Republican Wins of Democratic-Held Seats

Arkansas. Two-term senator Blanche Lincoln was decisively defeated, 58 percent to 37 percent, by John Boozman, a nine-year member of Congress from northwestern Arkansas. Lincoln, a political centrist, first drew a serious challenge from liberal lieutenant governor Bill Halter in the spring primary election after opposing some proposals endorsed by labor unions and the establishment of a government-run "public option" provision in a health care overhaul.

Though Lincoln managed to narrowly beat Halter in a runoff election, she began the general election campaign as a big underdog to Boozman, who had the advantages of running in a good Republican year and in a conservative-leaning state where Obama was very unpopular.

Illinois. In what was one of the Republican Party's most symbolic victories, representative Mark Steven Kirk defeated state treasurer Alexi Giannoulias, 48 percent to 46 percent, to claim the Senate seat once held by Barack Obama. Roland W. Burris was appointed to the seat after Obama became president, but he declined to run for a full term.

Illinois is a Democratic-leaning state, but Kirk became attractive to political independents and moderates after he carved out a centrist profile during a decade representing suburbs north of Chicago. He differs from most Republicans in being pro-choice and supporting embryonic stem cell research and an expansion of federal funding for children's health insurance.

Indiana. Former senator Dan Coats defeated Rep. Brad Ellsworth, 55 percent to 40 percent, and returned to the Senate twelve years after he ended his initial ten-year tenure (1989–1999). Coats will replace Evan Bayh, who succeeded Coats after the 1998 election and announced in February 2010 that he would not seek another term.

North Dakota. Gov. John Hoeven was overwhelmingly elected to the seat that three-term senator Byron Dorgan gave up upon retirement. Dorgan's retirement announcement in early 2010 was unexpected, though he may not have survived a matchup against Hoeven, a popular officeholder who won a third term as governor in 2008 with 74 percent of the vote. Hoeven exceeded even that lofty threshold in the Senate race, trouncing state senator Tracy Potter 76 percent to 22 percent.

> **FUN FACT**
>
> Indiana Republican Dan Coats, who was elected to the Senate seat he previously held from 1989 through 1999, will become the third former senator since 1913 to return to the Senate after an absence of twelve or more years. Theodore Burton, R-OH, left the Senate in March 1915 after one six-year term and returned in December 1928, nearly fourteen years later. James Hamilton Lewis, D-IL, served in the Senate from 1913 to 1919 and again from 1931 to 1939, an absence of twelve years.

Pennsylvania. Pat Toomey, a former three-term representative and conservative activist, defeated two-term representative Joe Sestak 51 to 49 percent. Toomey will succeed Arlen Specter, a former Republican who switched to the Democratic Party in April 2009. Specter made the switch after polls showed that he would lose to Toomey in a Republican primary. But a Toomey-Specter general election never happened because Specter was beaten in the Democratic primary by Sestak, who positioned himself as a more legitimate progressive Democrat.

Wisconsin. Three-term senator Russ Feingold lost 52 percent to 47 percent to Ron Johnson, the wealthy founder of a plastics manufacturing company and a first-time candidate for political office. Johnson was well-funded, ran with strong support from Tea Party activists, and touted his business background and lack of formal political experience—a major plus in an environment in which voters were looking for something fresh.

Republicans Hold All of Their Seats

Not only did Republicans wrest 6 Senate seats from the Democrats, they also won all eighteen contests in which Republicans were the defending party. None of the races were close: in each of the eighteen races, the Republican outpaced the Democrat by at least ten percentage points. In South Dakota, Democrats didn't even field a candidate against Sen. John Thune, who beat Tom Daschle six years earlier when Daschle was minority leader.

Here's a look at some of the major contests:

Alaska. Sen. Lisa Murkowski was re-elected in an unusual write-in campaign that she waged after losing the August Republican primary to Joe Miller, a lawyer and U.S. Army veteran. Strom Thurmond in 1954 is the only other person to win a Senate election through a write-in effort.

Conservative Tea Party activists hailed the election of Marco Rubio to the Senate. Rubio, a telegenic Florida Republican who previously served as a state House Speaker, is pictured here with his wife and four children at his victory celebration on November 2, 2010. Rubio easily defeated Gov. Charlie Crist, a longtime Republican who ran as an independent to avoid losing the Republican nomination to Rubio, and Democratic representative Kendrick Meek.

Florida. Former state House Speaker Marco Rubio won 49 percent of the vote in a three-way race that included Gov. Charlie Crist (30 percent), a Republican who ran as an independent, and Democratic representative Kendrick Meek (20 percent).

Crist seemed like a shoo-in for the seat when he announced in May 2009 that he would run for the seat of Republican Mel Martinez, who resigned after announcing his retirement. But Rubio whittled away at Crist's lead and eventually overtook the governor after he and Tea Party allies raised questions about Crist's conservative credentials, including his support for President Obama's economic stimulus plan.

Crist fell so far behind Rubio that he ultimately decided to run as an independent centrist candidate, positioning himself between the right-leaning Rubio and the left-leaning Meek. But with Rubio enjoying near-unanimous support among Republicans in a good Republican year, and Meek winning the votes of most black Democrats and some white liberals, it was difficult for Crist to carve out a path to victory. Rubio beat Crist by nearly twenty percentage points.

Kentucky. Rand Paul, an eye surgeon who is the son of Texas representative and 2008 presidential candidate Ron Paul, defeated state attorney general Jack Conway, 56 percent to 44 percent, to succeed retiring senator Jim Bunning.

Rand Paul, a first-time candidate for political office, was an early beneficiary of Tea Party activism, which propelled him to a victory in the primary over Trey

Grayson, the Kentucky secretary of state and preferred candidate of party establishment figures such as Senate minority leader Mitch McConnell.

Missouri. The Show Me State's new senator, Roy Blunt, served fourteen years as representative from the southwestern quadrant of the state before defeating Robin Carnahan, Missouri's secretary of state, 54 percent to 41 percent. Blunt's campaign and its Republican allies regularly referred to Carnahan as "Rubberstamp Robin," claiming that she sided too frequently with the positions of national Democratic Party leaders. Carnahan repeatedly pointed out Blunt's close ties to lobbyists, but the anti-Democratic political environment nationwide and in Missouri made it hard for her to gain traction.

New Hampshire. Kelly Ayotte, a former state attorney general, beat two-term representative Paul W. Hodes, 60 percent to 37 percent, to win the seat of retiring three-term senator Judd Gregg. Ayotte was the first woman to serve as New Hampshire's top legal officer and will serve with Democratic senator Jeanne Shaheen. New Hampshire is now one of four states with two female senators—California, Washington, and Maine are the others.

Ohio. Rob Portman, a former Cincinnati-area representative and later a top budget and trade official to President George W. Bush, trounced Lt. Gov. Lee Fisher, 57 percent to 39 percent, to succeed retiring two-term senator George Voinovich. Portman had a huge fund-raising advantage over Fisher and blamed his opponent, Ohio's "jobs czar," for the state's lagging economy. Portman's victory demonstrated the limits of the Democrats' strategy to tie Republican candidates to Bush, who was very unpopular at the tail end of his presidency.

Democrats Win Enough to Fend Off GOP Majority

Democrats managed to retain control of several seats targeted by the Republicans in their campaign to capture a Senate majority.

California. Barbara Boxer secured a fourth term against Carly Fiorina, a former Hewlett-Packard chief executive officer, in California's first-ever Senate race between two women. Some late surveys had Boxer and Fiorina in a toss-up contest, but Boxer won by a comfortable ten-point margin in part by painting Fiorina as too conservative for Democratic-leaning California and criticizing her actions as a business executive.

In the nation's most populous state, Republicans have lost eight consecutive Senate elections. Their last win came in 1988.

Connecticut. State attorney general Richard Blumenthal fended off a big-spending challenge from Linda McMahon, a former World Wrestling Entertainment chief executive, 55 percent to 43 percent. McMahon gave more than $50 million to her campaign.

Blumenthal will succeed Democrat Christopher Dodd, who retired after thirty years of Senate service.

Delaware. Chris Coons, the executive of New Castle County in Wilmington, easily defeated Christine O'Donnell, a perennial conservative candidate, for the seat that Joe Biden vacated after his election to the vice presidency.

As 2010 began, the general election contestants were expected not to be Coons and O'Donnell, but Democratic state attorney general Beau Biden, the vice president's eldest son, and Republican representative Mike Castle, a former governor and one of Delaware's most popular and enduring politicians.

Beau Biden announced in January that he would not run for the Senate, paving the way for Coons, an ambitious politician, to run as the Democratic nominee against Castle.

Unseating Castle was always a long shot proposition for Coons. But he was rewarded when Castle was surprisingly defeated in the Republican primary by the more conservative O'Donnell, who got the party nod despite strong opposition from Republican officials. Coons had no problem dispatching O'Donnell, 56 percent to 40 percent.

Nevada. Perhaps the Republicans' biggest regret of the 2010 campaign is that they blew a golden opportunity to unseat Senate majority leader Harry Reid, who was hampered by poor approval ratings in a state with the highest unemployment rate (14.4 percent in September 2010).

But Republicans nominated a flawed candidate in Sharron Angle, a former state legislator who had strong support from Tea Party activists. Reid portrayed her staunchly conservative views as too far out of the mainstream for Nevada, and he won by about five percentage points, stunning political analysts who expected him to become the first senate majority leader in fifty-eight years to lose a re-election campaign.

Washington. Sen. Patty Murray narrowly secured a fourth term, defeating Dino Rossi, a real estate businessman and twice-unsuccessful candidate for governor, 52 percent to 48 percent.

West Virginia. Gov. Joe Manchin was elected to the seat formerly held by Democrat Robert C. Byrd, the longest-serving senator in history who died in June 2010 at age 92. Manchin, a popular governor, beat Republican businessman John Raese 54 percent to 43 percent and is expected to seek a full six-year term in 2012.

Manchin typified a strategy used by many Democrats, which was to demonstrate their political independence from the Obama administration and congressional Democrats. A vigorous opponent of Obama's "cap and trade" legislation to curb greenhouse gases, Manchin aired a television commercial that showed him shooting at a copy of the bill with a rifle.

Some Senate Setbacks for Republicans

While the Republicans' 6-seat gain in 2010 was a clear success, there was some grumbling in some party quarters that Republicans didn't fully capitalize on one of the most favorable political environments in decades. In some states, Republicans may have hurt their chances to beat more Democrats because they had fractious primaries that pitted a candidate favored by Tea Party activists against a candidate backed by the party establishment.

This surely was the case in Delaware, where Republicans had long expected that veteran moderate representative Michael Castle would comfortably win the seat

A rare bright spot for Democrats on election night was the re-election of Senate majority leader Harry Reid in Nevada, where his poor approval rating and a sagging economy had made him vulnerable to defeat. Reid, shown here election night with his wife, Landra, overcame a determined challenge from Republican Sharron Angle, a former state legislator whom Reid painted as outside the political mainstream.

formerly held by Vice President Joe Biden. But Tea Party activists and former Alaska governor Sarah Palin wanted the Republican nominee to be the more conservative Christine O'Donnell, a twice-unsuccessful candidate for the Senate whose bizarre statements and personal financial trouble had given party leaders pause.

Tea Party activists also helped nominate Republicans in Colorado and Nevada over candidates backed by party establishment figures as more electable. In Colorado, county prosecutor Ken Buck won the Republican nomination over former lieutenant governor Jane Norton, the candidate favored by the National Republican Senatorial Committee. In Nevada, former state legislator Sharron Angle beat out Sue Lowden, a former chair of the Nevada Republican Party who was the early favorite for the Republican nomination. In the November balloting, Buck lost to Sen. Michael Bennet and Angle lost to Senate majority leader Harry Reid.

Utah Republican senator Robert Bennett, who was denied his party's nomination in the spring of 2010 in large part because of opposition by Tea Party activists, said that "by knocking off potentially electable nominees in Colorado, Delaware, and Nevada, they gave the Democrats the gift of three seats."[41]

Alabama Republican representative Spencer Bachus, the incoming chair of the Financial Services Committee, pointed a finger at the most prominent conservative activist of all. "Sarah Palin cost us control of the Senate," he told an Alabama audience November 4.[42]

TABLE 2
2010 U.S. Senate Election Results (36 Races)

State	Result	Incumbent
Alabama	Richard Shelby (R) 65%, Robert Barnes (D) 35%	Shelby
Alaska	Lisa Murkowski (Write-in) 39%, Joe Miller (R) 35%, Scott McAdams (D) 23%	Murkowski
Arizona	John McCain (R) 59%, Rodney Glassman (D) 35%	McCain
California	Barbara Boxer (D) 52%, Carly Fiorina (R) 42%	Boxer
Colorado	Michael Bennet (D) 48%, Ken Buck (R) 47%	Bennet
Connecticut	Richard Blumenthal (D) 55%, Linda McMahon (R) 43%	Christopher Dodd (D) did not seek re-election
Delaware	Chris Coons (D) 56%, Christine O'Donnell (R) 40%	Ted Kaufman (D) did not seek election
Florida	Marco Rubio (R) 49%, Charlie Crist (I) 30%, Kendrick Meek (D) 20%	George LeMieux (R) did not seek election
Georgia	Johnny Isakson (R) 58%, Mike Thurmond (D) 39%	Isakson
Hawaii	Daniel Inouye (D) 75%, Cam Cavasso (R) 21%	Inouye
Idaho	Michael Crapo (R) 71%, Tom Sullivan (D) 25%	Crapo
Illinois	Mark Kirk (R) 48%, Alexi Giannoulias (D) 46%	Roland Burris (D) did not seek election
Indiana	Dan Coats (R) 55%, Brad Ellsworth (D) 40%	Evan Bayh (D) did not seek re-election
Iowa	Chuck Grassley (R) 65%, Roxanne Conlin (D) 33%	Grassley
Kansas	Jerry Moran (R) 70%, Lisa Johnston (D) 26%	Sam Brownback (R) elected governor
Kentucky	Rand Paul (R) 56%, Jack Conway (D) 44%	Jim Bunning (R) did not seek re-election
Louisiana	David Vitter (R) 57%, Charlie Melancon (D) 38%	Vitter
Maryland	Barbara Mikulski (D) 62%, Eric Wargotz (R) 36%	Mikulski
Missouri	Roy Blunt (R) 54%, Robin Carnahan (D) 41%	Kit Bond (R) did not seek re-election
Nevada	Harry Reid (D) 50%, Sharron Angle (R) 45%	Reid
New Hampshire	Kelly Ayotte (R) 60%, Paul Hodes (D) 37%	Judd Gregg (R) did not seek re-election
New York	Charles Schumer (D) 65%, Jay Townsend (R) 33%	Schumer
New York	Kirsten Gillibrand (D) 62%, Joe DioGuardi (R) 36%	Gillibrand
North Carolina	Richard Burr (R) 55%, Elaine Marshall (D) 43%	Burr
North Dakota	John Hoeven (R) 76%, Tracy Potter (D) 22%	Byron Dorgan (D) did not seek re-election
Ohio	Rob Portman (R) 57%, Lee Fisher (D) 39%	George Voinovich (R) did not seek re-election
Oklahoma	Tom Coburn (R) 71%, Jim Rogers (D) 26%	Coburn
Oregon	Ron Wyden (D) 57%, Jim Huffman (R) 40%	Wyden
Pennsylvania	Pat Toomey (R) 51%, Joe Sestak (D) 49%	Arlen Specter (D) lost in the primary

State	Result	Incumbent
South Carolina	Jim DeMint (R) 62%, Alvin Greene (D) 28%	DeMint
South Dakota	John Thune (R) unopposed	Thune
Utah	Mike Lee (R) 61%, Sam Granato (D) 33%	Robert Bennett (R) lost at a nominating convention
Vermont	Patrick Leahy (D) 64%, Len Britton (R) 31%	Leahy
Washington	Patty Murray (D) 52%, Dino Rossi (R) 48%	Murray
West Virginia	Joe Manchin (D) 54%, John Raese (R) 43%	Carte Goodwin (D) did not seek election
Wisconsin	Ron Johnson (R) 52%, Russ Feingold (D) 47%	Feingold

Source: Compiled by the author.

Note: All won six-year terms except Gillibrand (NY), Manchin (WV), and Coons (DE), who won special elections. The terms of Gillibrand and Manchin expire at the end of 2012, and Coons's term expires at the end of 2014.

Gubernatorial Elections: Republicans Win a Majority

Republicans also were the big winners in the thirty-seven contests for governor on the 2010 ballot. The party netted six more governorships and will begin 2011 in control of twenty-nine of the fifty state executive mansions.

The 2010 midterm elections produced substantial turnover in governorships. In twenty-three contests the governor did not run for re-election, due to retirement or seeking other office or because term-limit laws precluded them from seeking new terms. Three governors were defeated for re-election, one in the primary election and two in the general election.

Republicans were elected to replace Democratic governors in eleven states: Iowa, Kansas, Maine, Michigan, New Mexico, Ohio, Oklahoma, Pennsylvania, Tennessee, Wisconsin, and Wyoming.

In Ohio, the nation's seventh most populous state, former U.S. representative John Kasich unseated Democratic incumbent Ted Strickland. Chet Culver of Iowa was the only other Democrat who was defeated for re-election; he lost to Terry Branstad, who was governor from 1983 to 1999.

The Republican campaign to win more governorships was aided by a strong showing by the party's political arm, the Republican Governors Association, which soundly outperformed its partisan counterpart, the Democratic Governors Association, in campaign fund-raising.

Democrats were elected to replace Republican governors in California, Connecticut, Hawaii, Minnesota, and Vermont—five states that President Obama won easily in the 2008 election. The Republican incumbents either retired or were barred by term limits from seeking re-election.

The biggest win for Democrats came in California, where state attorney general Jerry Brown defeated former eBay chief executive Meg Whitman, 53 percent to 41 percent, and won the job he previously held from 1975 to 1983. Brown, who ran for president three times and later served as mayor of Oakland, became the first person in history to win five million votes in a gubernatorial election.

Rhode Island elected an independent governor, Lincoln Chafee, who served in the U.S. Senate (1999–2007) as a liberal Republican and then later renounced his party affiliation. Maine nearly elected an independent governor, but lawyer Eliot Cutler fell just short to Republican winner Paul LePage.

The gubernatorial elections produced some important milestones for women. In New Mexico, Republican prosecutor Susana Martinez defeated another woman, Democratic lieutenant governor Diane Denish, to become the state's first female Republican governor and the first female Hispanic governor in U.S. history.

Republican women also were elected to governorships in South Carolina, where state representative Nikki Haley became the nation's first Indian-American female governor, and in Oklahoma, where U.S. representative Mary Fallin defeated Lt. Gov. Jeri Askins in the state's first-ever gubernatorial race between two women. Interestingly, South Carolina ranked fiftieth and Oklahoma forty-ninth among the fifty states in the share of state legislators who are women.[43]

Despite the election of Martinez, Haley, and Fallin, the number of female governors will remain unchanged at six. Linda Lingle, a Hawaii Republican; Jennifer Granholm, a Michigan Democrat; and Jodi Rell, a Connecticut Republican, did not seek re-election.

The 2010 election produced two Hispanic governors, Martinez and Nevada Republican Brian Sandoval, a former federal judge. Sandoval easily defeated Rory Reid, a county commissioner and a son of Senate majority leader Harry Reid.

The governors' races are important because the state chief executive officers shape budgetary policies, nominate judges, and perform other important executive tasks. In most states governors also have the power to influence the process of redrawing congressional lines that will ensue in the states before the 2012 elections.

State Legislatures

Republicans also significantly improved their standing in the nation's state legislatures, which will also have a major role in the redrawing of congressional district lines.

Republicans won control of at least twenty state legislative chambers from the Democrats and gained more than 675 state legislative seats overall, exceeding the 472-seat gain the party enjoyed in 1994. What was a 60–36 Democratic advantage in state legislatures became a 55–40 Republican edge. The nonpartisan National Conference on State Legislatures said the Republicans were in their best position in state legislatures since 1928.

Republicans won control of both the Alabama House and Alabama Senate, giving the party control of the legislature for the first time since Reconstruction. The Republicans also won control of the North Carolina Senate for the first time in 140 years and the Minnesota Senate for the first time ever.

TABLE 3
2010 Gubernatorial Election Results (37 Races)

State	Result	Incumbent
Alabama	Robert Bentley (R) 58%, Ron Sparks (D) 42%	Bob Riley (R)
Alaska	Sean Parnell (R) 59%, Ethan Berkowitz (D) 38%	Parnell
Arizona	Jan Brewer (R) 55%, Terry Goddard (D) 42%	Brewer
Arkansas	Mike Beebe (D) 64%, Jim Keet (R) 34%	Beebe
California	Jerry Brown (D) 54%, Meg Whitman (R) 41%	Arnold Schwarzenegger (R)
Colorado	John Hickenlooper (D) 51%, Tom Tancredo (I) 37%, Dan Maes (R) 11%	Bill Ritter (D)
Connecticut	Dan Malloy (D) 50%, Tom Foley (R) 49%	Jodi Rell (R)
Florida	Rick Scott (R) 49%, Alex Sink (D) 48%	Charlie Crist (R)
Georgia	Nathan Deal (R) 53%, Roy Barnes (D) 43%	Sonny Perdue (R)
Hawaii	Neil Abercrombie (D) 59%, Duke Aiona (R) 41%	Linda Lingle (R)
Idaho	Butch Otter (R) 59%, Keith Allred (D) 33%	Otter
Illinois	Pat Quinn (D) 46%, Bill Brady (R) 46%	Quinn
Iowa	Terry Branstad (R) 53%, Chet Culver (D) 43%	Culver
Kansas	Sam Brownback (R) 63%, Tom Holland (D) 32%	Mark Parkinson (D)
Maine	Paul LePage (R) 38%, Eliot Cutler (I) 37%, Libby Mitchell (D) 19%	John Baldacci (D)
Maryland	Martin O'Malley (D) 56%, Bob Ehrlich (R) 42%	O'Malley
Massachusetts	Deval Patrick (D) 49%, Charlie Baker (R) 42%	Patrick
Michigan	Rick Snyder (R) 58%, Virg Bernero (D) 40%	Jennifer Granholm (D)
Minnesota	Mark Dayton (D) 44%, Tom Emmer (R) 43%, Tom Horner (I) 12%	Tim Pawlenty (R)
Nebraska	Dave Heineman (R) 74%, Mike Meister (D) 26%	Heineman
Nevada	Brian Sandoval (R) 53%, Rory Reid (D) 41%	Jim Gibbons (R)
New Hampshire	John Lynch (D) 53%, John Stephen (R) 45%	Lynch
New Mexico	Susana Martinez (R) 54%, Diane Denish (D) 46%	Bill Richardson (D)
New York	Andrew Cuomo (D) 61%, Carl Paladino (R) 34%	David Paterson (D)
Ohio	John Kasich (R) 49%, Ted Strickland (D) 47%	Strickland
Oklahoma	Mary Fallin (R) 60%, Jari Askins (D) 40%	Brad Henry (D)
Oregon	John Kitzhaber (D) 49%, Chris Dudley (R) 48%	Ted Kulongoski (D)
Pennsylvania	Tom Corbett (R) 55%, Dan Onorato (D) 45%	Ed Rendell (D)
Rhode Island	Lincoln Chafee (I) 36%, John Robitaille (R) 34%, Paul Caprio (D) 23%	Don Carcieri (R)
South Carolina	Nikki Haley (R) 51%, Vincent Sheheen (D) 47%	Mark Sanford (R)
South Dakota	Dennis Daugaard (R) 62%, Scott Heidepriem (D) 38%	Mike Rounds (R)
Tennessee	Jim Haslam (R) 65%, Mike McWherter (D) 33%	Phil Bredesen (D)
Texas	Rick Perry (R) 55%, Bill White (D) 42%	Perry
Utah	Gary Herbert (R) 64%, Pete Corroon (D) 32%	Herbert
Vermont	Peter Shumlin (D) 50%, Brian Dubie (R) 48%	Jim Douglas (R)
Wisconsin	Scott Walker (R) 52%, Tom Barrett (D) 47%	Jim Doyle (D)
Wyoming	Matt Mead (R) 72%, Leslie Petersen (D) 25%	Dave Freudenthal (D)

Source: Compiled by the author.

Five Reasons Why Democrats Lost

Reason #1: The Economy

There is no doubt that the flagging economy was the dominant issue in the 2010 campaign and a major factor contributing to Democratic losses and Republican gains. As the governing party in control of the White House, the House, and the Senate, Democrats bore the brunt of voter anger at a time when the economy was not improving as quickly as hoped.

The unemployment rate in October 2010 was 9.6 percent, higher than the 7.7 percent rate in January 2009 and the fifteenth consecutive month that the rate was 9.5 percent or higher—the longest such period of high unemployment since the Great Depression.

According to a national exit poll of the 2010 election, 63 percent said that the economy was the most important issue in the election, and 61 percent said the country was on the "wrong track." Eighty-six percent of respondents said that they were worried about economic conditions; they voted Republican by a margin of 57 percent to 39 percent.[44]

The poor economy pulled down Obama's approval rating from the low 60s early in his presidency to the mid-to-high 40s before the midterm elections. Obama's standing was comparable to Bill Clinton's approval rating just before the 1994 elections, when Republicans also made large seat gains. Obama's approval rating also is close to Ronald Reagan's in 1982, when his Republican Party lost 26 seats in the House amid an economic recession.

Reason #2: Voter Skepticism toward Obama's Policies

The Obama administration and the Democratic Congress enacted an array of new laws to boost the economy, including an $814 billion economic stimulus package, a health care overhaul, and a financial regulations package that aimed to rein in the excesses of Wall Street firms.

But most of the voting public was not convinced these policies would work. According to a national exit poll of the November election, just 32 percent of respondents said that Obama's stimulus program helped the economy, compared to 34 percent who said it hurt the economy and 31 percent who said it made no difference.[45]

"It goes to what many people see as the paradox of the Obama presidency: extraordinary legislative achievements, historical in their magnitude, but seemingly no thanks from the public. To the contrary, a public deeply skeptical," Brookings Institution political scientist Thomas E. Mann told *Congressional Quarterly* a few weeks before the election.[46]

In addition, it was very difficult for Obama and his Democratic allies to promote the health care law, a complicated piece of legislation that does not kick in fully for a few years.

Former president Bill Clinton said in August 2009 that "the minute the president signs the health care reform bill, approval will go up because Americans are inherently

FIGURE 1
Obama Job Approval

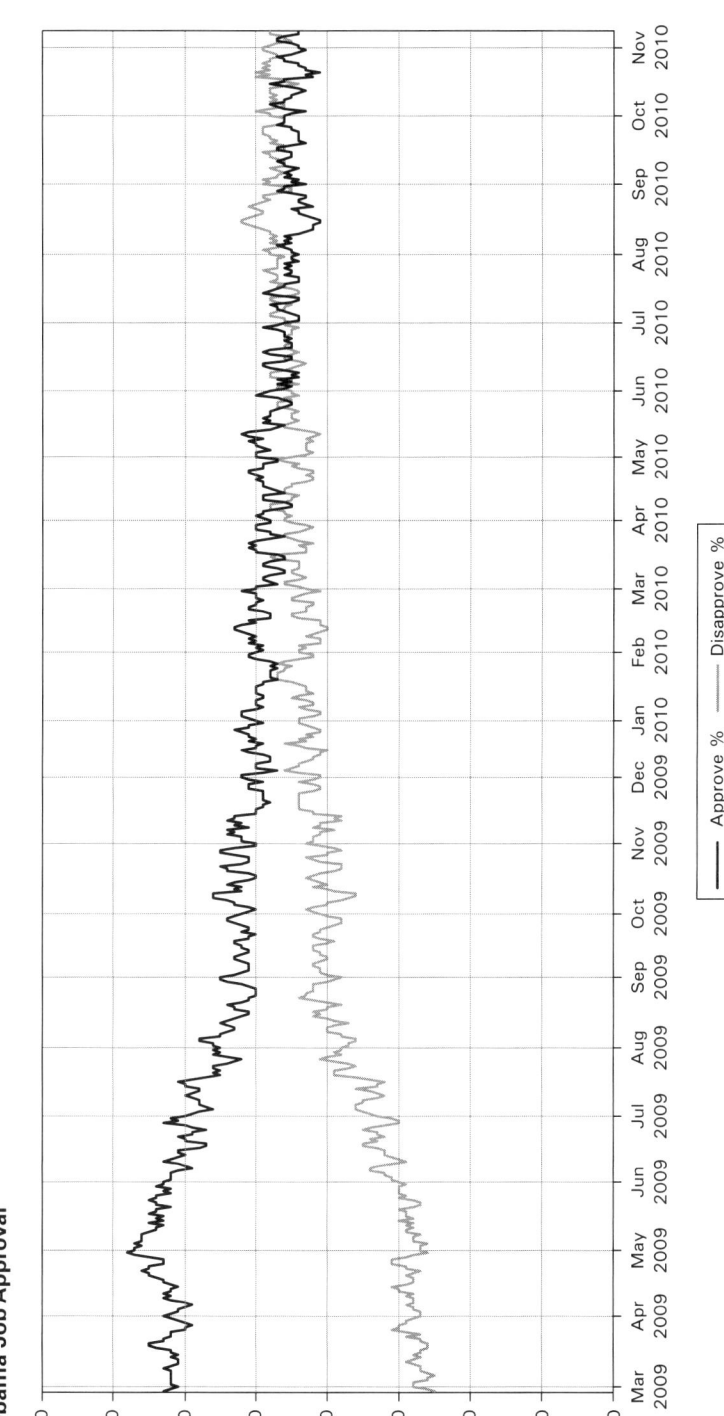

Source: Copyright © 2010 Gallup, Inc. All rights reserved. "Gallup Daily: Obama Job Approval" 2009–2010. Link: http://www.gallup.com/poll/113980/Gallup-Daily-Obama-Job-Approval.aspx?version=print.

Notes: Each result is based on a three-day rolling average. Gallup tracks daily the percentage of Americans who approve or disapprove of the job Barack Obama is doing as president. Results are based on telephone interviews with approximately 1,500 adults; margin of error is three percentage points.

FIGURE 2
Unemployment Rate

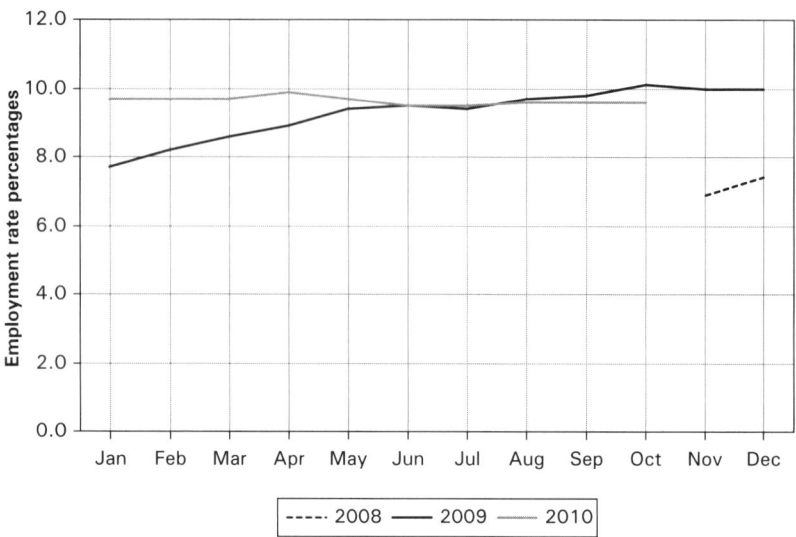

Source: U.S. Department of Labor, Bureau of Labor Statistics, "Labor Force Statistics from the Current Population Survey," Series ID: LNS14000000. Available at http://data.bls.gov/PDQ/servlet/SurveyOutputServlet?data_tool=latest_numbers&series_id=LNS14000000.

optimistic." Yet thirteen months later, Clinton said on NBC's *Meet the Press* program that he was "wrong about that [prediction] for two reasons."

"First of all, the benefits of the bill are spread out over three or four years. It takes a long time to implement it. And secondly, there was—there's been an enormous and highly effective attack on it," Clinton said.[47]

Reason #3: History and the "Enthusiasm Gap"

At the beginning of the election cycle, there was no doubt that the Democrats would lose seats. History says so: in nearly every midterm election since the Civil War, the party in the White House has lost ground in Congress.

One reason for this trend is that the energy and enthusiasm tends to be with the out-of-power party. Opponents of a new president are eager to vote in a midterm election as a way of "sending a message" to the White House.

A Gallup poll conducted September 20–26 carried an early warning sign for Democrats. According to the survey, 48 percent of self-identified Republicans said they were "very enthusiastic" about voting in the midterm elections, compared to just 28 percent of Democrats.

"Generally speaking, the party whose identifiers show an advantage on voting enthusiasm tends to fare better on Election Day," Gallup said.[48]

Obama tried to energize Democrats by portraying the election as a choice between Democratic policies he said improved the economy and a Republican plan he said

TABLE 4
Presidential Job Approval and U.S. House Seat Change in Midterm Elections, from Truman to Obama

Year	President/Political party	% Approval	Seat gain/loss in U.S. House for president's party
2010	Obama/Democrat**	43	−63 (as of Nov. 23, 2010)
2006	G.W. Bush/Republican	38	−30
2002	G.W. Bush/Republican	63	6
1998	Clinton/Democrat	66	5
1994	Clinton/Democrat	46	−53
1990	G.H.W. Bush/Republican	58	−8
1986	Reagan/Republican	63	−5
1982	Reagan/Republican	42	−28
1978	Carter/Democrat	49	−11
1974	Ford/Republican*	54	−43
1970	Nixon/Republican	58	−12
1966	Johnson/Democrat	44	−47
1962	Kennedy/Democrat	61	−4
1958	Eisenhower/Republican	57	−47
1954	Eisenhower/Republican	61	−18
1950	Truman/Democrat	39	−29
1946	Truman/Democrat	33	−55

Source: Copyright © 2010 Gallup, Inc. All rights reserved. "Understanding Gallup's Election 2010 Key Indicator" 1946–2010. http://www.gallup.com/poll/127982/Understanding-Gallup-Election-2010-Key-Indicators.aspx.
*Ford took office less than three months before the midterm elections, replacing Richard Nixon, who had 24% approval when he resigned. **Obama data from October 31–November 2, 2010.

would endanger the country's fragile recovery. Obama and Democratic National Committee chair Tim Kaine frequently charged on the campaign trail that Republicans drove the economy into "a ditch."

"It is inexcusable for any Democrat or progressive right now to stand on the sidelines in this midterm election," Obama told *Rolling Stone* magazine in a September 2010 interview. "There may be complaints about us not having gotten certain things done, not fast enough, making certain legislative compromises. But right now, we've got a choice between a Republican Party that has moved to the right of George Bush and is looking to lock in the same policies that got us into these disasters in the first place, versus an administration that, with some admitted warts, has been the most successful administration in a generation in moving progressive agendas forward."

"We have to get folks off the sidelines. People need to shake off this lethargy, people need to buck up," the president said.[49]

Yet by election day, Republicans were clearly more eager to vote than Democrats. According to the final *USA Today*/Gallup pre-election poll, conducted October 28–31, 63 percent of respondents who were Republican or leaned Republican said they were "more enthusiastic than usual" about voting in the midterm election. Just 44 percent of Democrats said the same.

"The high level of Republican enthusiasm has led to the largest gap in enthusiasm by party of any recent midterm elections, 19 percentage points," Gallup said. "The prior highs were nine points in favor of the Democrats in 2006, and nine points in favor of the Republicans in 1994."[50]

Comparing the aggregate vote for Democratic and Republican U.S. House candidates confirms the enthusiasm gap. Voter turnout always is lower in midterm elections than in higher-profile presidential elections, but the drop-off in votes for Democrats was dramatic. In 2008 House races, Democrats won 65.2 million votes; in 2010, they won about 38 million votes, a 42 percent decline. The Republican drop-off was modest, from 52.2 million votes in 2008 to 44.2 million in 2010, a 15 percent decline.

The midterm election voting pool was older, whiter, and more conservative than the electorate in 2008, when young voters and African Americans in particular turned out in large numbers to propel Obama and Democrats to victory. In 2008, first-time voters comprised 11 percent of the voting pool and broke heavily for Obama; in 2010, just 3 percent of voters were casting a ballot for the first time.

Reason #4: Failure to Communicate

Democrats faltered in convincing the electorate about their accomplishments. A *Bloomberg News* national poll taken October 24–26, 2010, showed that most voters thought that taxes had gone up, the economy had shrunk, and most of the money spent under the Troubled Asset Relief Program (TARP) to assist banks had been lost. In each case, the facts showed otherwise.

"The public view of the economy is at odds with the facts, and the blame has to go to the Democrats," said J. Ann Selzer, the president of Selzer & Company, the polling firm that conducted the survey. "It does not matter much if you make change, if you do not communicate change."[51]

"The administration has said for a long time that the best politics was doing the right thing," said Steve McMahon, a Democratic strategist. "It requires a lot more. These numbers show that the best politics is selling what you're doing."[52]

Obama said shortly before the election that "one of the challenges we had two years ago was we had to move so fast, we were in such emergency mode that it was very difficult for us to spend a lot of time doing victory laps and advertising exactly what we were doing."

"I take some responsibility for that," Obama added.[53]

Reason #5: Outside Spending

Republicans would have outperformed Democrats even if the GOP had not been aided by significant fund-raising among conservative organizations that aired television advertisements attacking Democrats. But the extra assistance clearly helped Republicans win more races than they would have otherwise. Republican-leaning groups spent $167 million between September 1 and October 31 in support of their party's nominees, compared with $68 million spent by Democratic-leaning organizations.[54]

These Republican-leaning outside groups felt compelled to influence the midterm elections in part because Republican Party organizations lagged behind their Democratic counterparts in fund-raising. The Republican National Committee in particular

The 2010 election was characterized by an influx of spending from outside groups, some of which were permitted to raise unlimited sums of money without disclosing their donors. This television advertisement attacking Senate majority leader Harry Reid, a Nevada Democrat, was aired by Crossroads Grassroots Policy Strategies, an advocacy group with ties to Karl Rove and other Republican officials.

had a subpar fund-raising performance under the leadership of Michael Steele, whose gaffes created a distraction for the party's political efforts. Big-money donors who were hesitant to give to the RNC gave to these outside groups instead.

The most prominent groups included a pair of organizations, American Crossroads and Crossroads Grassroots Public Strategies (GPS), that were conceived by Karl Rove, a former senior adviser to President George W. Bush, and Ed Gillespie, a former chief of staff to Bush who also served as chair of the Republican National Committee.

Americans Crossroads is organized as a "527" political organization, identified by the section of the federal tax code under which it incorporates. 527 committees can accept unlimited contributions to spend on political advertisements, though they cannot coordinate their campaign efforts with preferred candidates.

Crossroads GPS organized as a tax-exempt 501c4 organization that is supposed to be primarily engaged in social welfare. Though there are limits to the political activities a 501c4 group can engage in, the advantage to forming such a group is that it does not have to disclose its donors—guaranteeing privacy to big donors who don't want their contributions to be vetted by the media or political opponents.

Sen. Max Baucus, a Montana Democrat who heads the tax-writing Finance Committee, wrote the Internal Revenue Service in late September to ask it to survey major 501c organizations involved in political campaign activity "to examine whether they are operated for the organization's intended tax exempt purpose and to ensure that political campaign activity is not the organization's primary activity."[55]

The Democrats also trained their fire on the U.S. Chamber of Commerce, the large business federation that traditionally supports more Republicans than Democrats. Senior Democrats accused the organization of spending money on the midterm elections that had been raised from foreign sources, though they could not provide any proof of the allegations.

"I challenge the Chamber of Commerce to tell us how much of the money they're investing is from foreign sources," Vice President Biden said October 11 during a campaign stop in Pennsylvania. "I challenge them. If I'm wrong, I will stand corrected." Tom Collamore, the Chamber's senior vice president of communications and strategy, responded, "Not a single cent."[56]

Republican operatives dismissed the complaints as baseless and noted that Democratic-leaning organizations, aided by labor unions and wealthy liberals like financier George Soros, spent hundreds of millions of dollars on the 2008 election.

Outside groups should play a major role in the 2012 elections, when Obama presumably will be seeking re-election and Democrats will be looking to save their majority in the Senate and win back the majority in the House. Absent any new restrictions on the financing of campaigns, the 2012 campaign might become the most expensive in history.

The next election is never far off the minds of officeholders, even immediately after the past election. President Obama will soon begin formal preparations for his expected re-election campaign, and he will want to run on a platform of delivering the change he promised during the 2008 campaign but which most voters say they haven't felt. Republicans running the U.S. House, mindful that voters have given them a second chance after four years in the minority, want to earn the trust of an electorate that doesn't think highly of either major political party. Democrats in the Senate will want to set their own marker, too, and do everything they can to prevent the Republicans from winning control of the chamber.

Obama and congressional Democrats and Republicans all have some incentive to work together. A restive and frustrated public demands it. The 2010 elections were a clear sign that we live in a politically volatile time, and federal officeholders realize that many of them could lose their jobs in the 2012 election if they don't produce results. But compromise may be elusive and gridlock the norm on more issues than not, given the vast gap in governing philosophies between a mostly liberal Democratic Party and a strongly conservative Republican Party that is eager to undo Obama's policies. It will be interesting to see to what extent the two sides will try to work together over the next two years, amid the political pressures of the 2012 presidential campaign, to solve the nation's problems.

Notes

1. Obama remarks at press conference, November 3, 2010. Accessed at www.whitehouse.gov/the-press-office/2010/11/03/press-conference-president.
2. Obama press availability aboard Air Force One, November 14, 2010.

3. "A Clear Rejection of the Status Quo, No Consensus about Future Policies," Pew Research Center for the People and the Press, November 3, 2010. Accessed at http://pewresearch.org/pubs/1789/2010-midterm-elections-exit-poll-analysis.
4. Rubio national Republican radio address, November 6, 2010.
5. "Historic Wins for Idaho Republicans," KTRV-TV, November 3, 2010. Accessed at www.fox12idaho.com/Global/story.asp?S=13442255.
6. Chris Cillizza, "Did the 'Pledge to America' Work?" The *Washington Post*'s "The Fix" blog, November 16, 2010. Accessed at http://voices.washingtonpost.com/thefix/house/did-the-pledge-to-america-work.html.
7. The AP-GfK Poll, conducted November 3-8, 2010. Available at http://surveys.ap.org.
8. Duberstein interviewed on Bloomberg Television, October 15, 2010.
9. *USA Today*/Gallup Poll conducted November 4–7, 2010. Available at www.gallup.com/poll/File/144356/Election_Aftermath_Nov_10_2010.pdf.
10. Issa appearance on *Fox News Sunday,* November 7, 2010.
11. Author notes from a post-election conference November 4, 2010, that was hosted by the Greater Washington Board of Trade.
12. John Rossomando, "Republicans Plan January Takedowns of Obama's 'Czars,'" *Daily Caller,* October 14, 2010.
13. See Senate Roll Call Vote 395, December 23, 2009, and Senate Roll Call Vote 396, December 24, 2009. Accessed at www.senate.gov/legislative/LIS/roll_call_lists/vote_menu_111_1.htm.
14. Obama's weekly address, November 6, 2010. Accessed at www.whitehouse.gov/the-press-office/2010/11/06/weekly-address-president-obama-calls-compromise-and-explains-his-priorit.
15. Bloomberg National Poll, conducted October 7–10, 2010, of 721 likely voters by Selzer & Company. Margin of error is plus or minus 3.7 percentage points.
16. The AP-GfK Poll, conducted November 3–8, 2010. Available at http://surveys.ap.org.
17. Kaiser Health Tracking Poll, October 2010. Accessed at www.kff.org/kaiserpolls/upload/8115-F.pdf.
18. Interview of President Obama by *National Journal*'s Ron Fournier and Ronald Brownstein, October 19, 2010. Transcript available at www.nationaljournal.com/whitehouse/complete-transcript-of-obama-interview-20101024.
19. Senate majority leader Harry Reid (D-NV) interviewed on CNN, November 3, 2010.
20. Robert Pear, "G.O.P. to Fight Health Law with Purse Strings," *New York Times,* November 6, 2010.
21. Executive Order 13531, National Commission on Fiscal Responsibility and Reform, signed February 18, 2010. Accessed at http://edocket.access.gpo.gov/2010/pdf/2010-3725.pdf.
22. Obama news conference in Seoul, South Korea, November 11, 2010.
23. Nicholas Johnston, "Obama Says Arms Treaty 'Imperative' for U.S. Security," *Bloomberg News,* November 18, 2010.
24. Peter Baker, "Obama Forces Showdown with G.O.P. on Arms Pact," *New York Times,* November 19, 2010. Available at www.nytimes.com/2010/11/19/world/europe/19start.html.
25. Obama's 2010 State of the Union address, January 27, 2010. Text available at www.whitehouse.gov/the-press-office/remarks-president-state-union-address.
26. Duberstein interviewed on Bloomberg Television, October 15, 2010.
27. CQ–Roll Call Group's "Election Impact" conference, November 4, 2010.
28. "Public Support for Increased Trade, Except with South Korea and China," Pew Research Center for the People and the Press, November 9, 2010. Report available at http://people-press.org/report/673.
29. Roger Runningen and Angela Greiling Keane, "Obama Says 'Crumbling' Infrastructure Hinders Growth," *Bloomberg News,* October 11, 2010.
30. Author's notes from a November 4, 2010, post-election briefing in Washington, D.C., that was sponsored by the Greater Washington Board of Trade.

31. John Lauerman, "Education's Duncan Working with Boehner on 'No Child,'" *Bloomberg News*, November 16, 2010.
32. John Lauerman and Nicholas Johnston, "Obama Job Strategy Backs Two-Year Colleges, Attacks Republicans," *Bloomberg News*, October 6, 2010.
33. N.J. interview, see later cite.
34. Jeffrey M. Jones, "Views of GOP's Ability to Govern Similar to 1994, 2006," Gallup, October 7, 2010. Accessed at www.gallup.com/poll/143459/Views-GOP-Ability-Govern-Similar-1994-2006.aspx.
35. Larry J. Sabato, "Sixty Days to Go: The Crystal Ball's Labor Day Predictions," September 2, 2010. Available at www.centerforpolitics.org/crystalball/articles/ljs2010090201.
36. Charlie Cook, "The GOP Wave Keeps Coming," *National Journal*'s *CongressDaily/AM*, September 28, 2010.
37. Alex Isenstadt, "Van Hollen Defends DCCC Efforts in Exit Memo," *Politico*, November 18, 2010.
38. Jonathan Martin, "Top RNC Aide Quits, Blasts Michael Steele," *Politico*, November 16, 2010.
39. Ben Wolfgang, "Holden Says Pelosi Is Responsible for Democrats' Losses, Should Step Down as Party Leader," *Pottsville Republican-Herald*, November 6, 2010.
40. Jonathan Allen and Jake Sherman, "Nancy Pelosi Survives Democratic Revolt," *Politico*, November 17, 2010.
41. Sen. Robert Bennett (R-Utah), "2010 Was the Year of Two Elections," *The Hill*, November 15, 2010. Accessed at http://thehill.com/opinion/op-ed/129285-2010-was-the-year-of-two-elections.
42. Jan Griffey, "Spencer Bachus: Sarah Palin Cost GOP Control of U.S. Senate," *Shelby County Reporter*, November 7, 2010.
43. Statistics from the Center for American Women and Politics at Rutgers University, www.cawp.rutgers.edu.
44. National U.S. House exit poll available at www.cnn.com/ELECTION/2010/results/polls/#val=USH00p1.
45. Ibid.
46. Bob Benenson, "Democratic Accomplishments: That Was Them," *CQ Weekly*, October 11, 2010, page 2340.
47. NBC's *Meet the Press*, September 19, 2010. Transcript available at www.msnbc.msn.com/id/39235412/ns/meet_the_press-transcripts.
48. Frank Newport, "Midterm Election Landscape Still Points to Republican Gains," Gallup, September 27, 2010. Accessed at www.gallup.com/poll/143243/Midterm-Election-Landscape-Points-Republican-Gains.aspx.
49. Jann S. Wenner, "Obama in Command: The Rolling Stone Interview," *Rolling Stone*, October 15, 2010. Accessed at www.rollingstone.com/politics/news/17390/209395.
50. Jeffrey M. Jones, "Record Midterm Enthusiasm as Voters Head to Polls," Gallup, November 2, 2010. Available at www.gallup.com/poll/144152/record-midterm-enthusiasm-voters-head-polls.aspx.
51. Heidi Przybyla and John McCormick, "Poll Shows Voters Don't Know GDP Grew with Tax Cuts," *Bloomberg News*, October 29, 2010.
52. Ibid.
53. Obama remarks at campaign event in Seattle, Washington, October 21, 2010.
54. Jonathan D. Salant and Traci McMillan, "Rove Groups, U.S. Chamber Build Winning Record in Elections," *Bloomberg News*, November 4, 2010.
55. Kenneth P. Vogel, "Baucus Seeks Probe of GOP Groups," *Politico*, September 29, 2010. Accessed at www.politico.com/news/stories/0910/42882.html.
56. Meredith Shiner, "Chamber of Commerce to Joe Biden: 'Not a Single Cent'" *Politico*, October 11, 2010. Accessed at www.politico.com/news/stories/1010/43446.html.